THE
KEY
OF
DAVID

THADDEUS LOCKHART

authorHOUSE®

AuthorHouse™
1663 Liberty Drive
Bloomington, IN 47403
www.authorhouse.com
Phone: 1 (800) 839-8640

Published by AuthorHouse 06/01/2020

ISBN: 978-1-7283-6292-2 (sc)
ISBN: 978-1-7283-6291-5 (e)

Print information available on the last page.

Scripture quotations marked NKJV are taken from the New King James Version. Copyright © 1982 by Thomas Nelson, Inc. Used by permission. All rights reserved.

This book is printed on acid-free paper.

CONTENTS

"These things says He who is holy, He who is true, He who has the key of David, He who opens and no one shuts and shuts and no one opens." (Rev. 3.7).

DEDICATION

This book is Dedicated to the elect lady and her children, whom I "respect," in the truth; and not I only, but also all they that have known the truth,"(2 Jn. 1.1)

THE AUTHOR

I am "Thaddeus Michael Lebbeus," I was born Thaddeus Michael Lockhart, shortly after Israel became a nation (3-14-1948) on October 18, 1948 (Tishri 15, 5709).

On January 18, 1976 when I was 27 years of age while I was watching Superbowl 10, on television, the Spirit of God descended upon me and caused the psychic phenomenon that upset game and shocked the world when the voice from heaven said. "This is my beloved Son in whom I am well pleased, hear him." (Mt. 17.5).

Shortly thereafter I was falsely accused, illegally convicted and sentence to 45 years at the Eastham Unit of the Texas prison system, where I reduced the revelations I received into writings.

"The key of David," follows and (1) reveals the true historical Jesus Christ, (2) shows how he overcame death by crucifixion and lived on to dictate the contents of the New Testament's gospels, the epistles and the Book of

Revelation, and prepared the mystery of the return of the Spirit of God in the Messiah Thaddeus, who "will guide you into all truth." (John 16.13).

The wise choose leaders who inspire others unto their own greatness.

Thaddeus Michael Lebbeus

PREFACE

"The Key of David,"

The Hebrew name "David," (H1732) comes from the Hebrew root word dhodh (H1730) which is a pun of the Egyptian public name "Thoth," who sacred hidden name was "Yah." The name "Thoth," appears in the Hebrew name "Anathoth," among the list of cities assigned to the priests, the Essene's Order of Melchizedek, who hid the truth of these things in the Bible. The Essene's Order of Melchizedek used the names of the thirteen cities given to the Leviticus priests to secretly describe themselves and the location of the sacred city called "Shiloh," to which the Holy One of God must come "spiritually and intellectually. Hence, the Key of David, is the key of Thoth, i.e. whose sacred hidden name was "Yah," (Jah), i.e. the key of Life.

(Gen. 49.10; Josh. 21.13-19). The writers knew that the Old Testament writings would someday be translated or changed, but one names are transliterated and have a discoverable meaning which a communicate as follows.

City's Name	Meaning
Hebron (H-2275)	Alliance
Libnah (H-3841)	Purity
Jattir (H-3492)	Pre-eminent
Eshtemoa (H-851)	Obedience
Holon (H-2473)	Cave
Debir (H-1687)	Sanctuary
Ayin (H-5867)	Eyes
Juttah (H-3194)	Extended
Beth-Shemesh(H-1053)	Egyptian Temple of God
Gibeon (H-1391)	Hill city
Giba (H-1388)	Hill
Anathoth (H-6068)	Anathoth
Almon (H-5960)	Hidden

The names of these priestly cities' communication to the adept initiates.

"(Priestly) alliance of purity per-eminent in obedience of cave sanctuary, whose eyes are extended to the Ancient Egyptian temple of God, has a (sacred) hill city in hill of Anathoth hidden."

In the final, analysis "the Key of David," is "the key of Thoth," whose sacred hidden name was "Yah," (Jah), which denotes "life," and reveals the Key of David is "the key of Life," (the key of the living God), and the key of Thaddeus, who will guide you into all truth." (John 16.13).

Chapter 1

THE LIFE OF JESUS CHRIST, THE TRUE STORY

"Jesus Christ," was born, the biological son of "Mariamne, II" (Mary), the virgin daughter of a priest name "Simeon," (the Oppressed virgin) and king Herod (the Oppressor) who sexually defiled her, who was "betrothed to marry Joseph of Arimathea," (Mt. 1.18; 27.57-61).

King Herod sexual defilement of "Mariamne, II," compelled her to marry him by law. To appease the anger of her father Simeon anger and the anger of the Jews, King Herod made Mariamne II's father Simeon, high priest, and ordered the rebuilding of the temple. (Dan. 9.25, 26: Lk. 2.22-24).

When Mariamne II (Mary) was about six (6) months when she could no longer hide her pregnancy from King Herod (busy with rebuilding project), she left to visit her cousin Elizabeth and remained there three (3) months until she (Mariamne II) gave birth to "baby Jesus," and left him to be raised by the elderly Zacharias and Elizabeth under the name "John," and Zacharias and Elizabeth cared for the Christ-child (John) until he underwent his "bar mitzvah," and was accepted into the Essenes' Order of Melchizedek at 13 years old (Lk. 2.41-50).

However, he only studied under them about two years, until he learned he was the son of King Herod, who had just ordered his mother "Mariamne II," (Mary) be murder in early 4 B.C. before his death.

This led the 15-year-old "Jesus," (John) making his first violently attempt to seize the throne of Judea as "Theudas," in 4 B.C. date supplied by Matthew's story alludes to Joseph rescuing Mariamne II (Mary) and taking her (Jesus' mother) to Egypt until Herod died, (Mt. 2.1f; Acts 5.36)

Luke's 6 A.D. date for Jesus birth, alludes to when Jesus under the name "Judas of Galilee," made a second failed attempt to violently seize the throne in about 6 A.D., "during taxing," when he was about 25-26 years old. (Lk. 2.1, 2; Acts 5.37).

Thereafter, the failed "Judas of Galilee attempt Jesus went into seclusion in wilderness for a 18-year period of time, during which he studied the scriptural writings, formulated a course of action and thereafter re-surfaced "John, the Baptist, John the Baptist appeared looking to baptize the coming "Messiah," using the words of Psalm

2.7, when the Spirit of God descended upon him "Jesus," (John) and heaven declared he (John) was God's Son. (Mt. 3.17; Mk. 1.11; 3.22; Zech. 4.9; 6.13; 4.14; Rev.11.14), and was compel to once again change his identity from "John, the Baptist," to "Jesus Christ," who took leadership of the disciples of John, and they John's disciples immediately followed him without question because they knew their master despite the change in appearance.

At the beginning of his ministry when Jesus Christ cleaned out the temple, the Jews asked "What sign do you show to us since you do these things?" and Jesus said "Destroy this temple, and in three days I will raise it up." Then the Jews said, it has taken forty-six (46) years to build this temple and will you raise it up in three days?" But he was speaking of the temple of his body." (John 2.18-21). The Jews asked him "What sign do you show to us, since you do these things?", and Christ Jesus said to them, "Destroy this temple, and in three days I will raise it up. (John 2.19), but he was speaking of the temple of his body.

Therefore, when he (Jesus) had risen from the dead, his disciples remembered that he had said this to them and they believed the Scripture, and the word which Jesus had said." (John 2.18, 19-22; Mt. 16.12). The disciples and the disciples of the disciples said that Jesus was 46 years when he held the office of teacher because they knew he was born when the temple was rebuilt. (comp. John 8.57).

Jesus asked "Who do men say that I, the Son of Man

am?" and their response was that Some say "John, the Baptist, some Elijah, and others Jeremiah or one of the prophets.

However, when he asked his disciples who they said he was Peter declared "You are the Christ, the Son of the living God," then he gave Peter the keys, and commanded his disciples that they should tell no one that he was Jesus, the Christ." (Mt. 16.13-20). Because he had assumed the spiritual identity of "the Son of man," (false-Christ), to destroy the work of the devil.

The term "the Son of man," is a spiritual description of the false Christ (Messiah) of the Great Synagogue identified as "Son of Adam," who was to be a human sacrifice for sins unto their called "Jehovah," (the Lord). The facts suggest the true Messiah (the Son of God) came and assumed the "Son of man," false-Christ identity who was to a human sacrifice for sins. (comp. Lk. 4.18; 2 Thes. 2.4).

After telling them he was presenting himself as "the Son of man," Christ Jesus (the Son of God) "he (Jesus) began to teach them, that "the Son of man," must be rejected, killed, and raised on third day. (Mk. 8.31).

Shortly thereafter Jesus is said to had with into the mountain and transfigured himself and appeared as the (Messiah) Moses because he was the true Messiah (Christ), and also showed himself as the "Elijah," who would come before great and dreadful day of the Lord."

(Mal. 4.5). To show himself as the Messiah Moses and to show he was in fact the Messiah (the Son of God) but also showed himself as the Elijah, who was to come before the day of the Lord because he was not presenting himself as "the "Messiah," (the Son of God), at that time, but he was presenting himself as "the Son of man."

The Jesus intentionally represented himself as "the Son of man," character who is identified with "the son of perdition," (comp. Lk. 4.18-21; 2Thes. 2.3f), to destroy the word of the devil (1 Jn. 3.8). and restore the ancient prophecy.

Chapter 2

THE CRUCIFIXION AND RESURRECTION

"From that time Jesus began to show to his disciples that he (the Son of man) must go to Jerusalem, and suffer many things from the elders and chief priests and scribes, be killed, and be raised the third day." (Mt. 16.21). Then Jesus himself said to his disciples:

"Assuredly, I say to you, there are some (disciples) standing here who shall not taste death till they see the Son of Man coming in his kingdom." (Mt. 16.28).

No two ways about it, Jesus either returned as he said he would, "before all the apostles died or he lied?"

When Jesus was being arrested, tried, and sentenced to be crucified, many women from Galilee "followed him looking from afar," among whom were "Mary Magdalene," and (third)"Mary the mother of James, the less, Joses, and

Salome," (Mk. 15.40, 41; Mt. 2&.55, 56). Elsewhere, Mary mother of James, (the less), and Joses, (Mt. 27.56).

In Mark, Mary Magdalene, sees a young man clothes in a long white garment. (Mk. 16.5) In Matthew they see "the angel of the Lord," whose countenance was like lighting and his raiment white as snow. (Mt. 28.2, 3); John says "Mary Magdalene" stood down and looked into the tomb and saw "two angels," in white," (John 20.11, 12). Luke there appeared "two men stood by them in shing garments.

(Luke 24.4), who are commonly identified as "angels." Taken in context, the Gospel of Luke, was the last written gospel.

On the way to the cross one of the soldiers gave Jesus "sour wine," mingled with gall to drink, but when Jesus tasted it, he would not drink it and they proceeded to nail him to the cross. (Mt. 27.34). There were four persons standing by the cross of Jesus, i.e. "the disciple whom Jesus loved, and 'three different females all named (1). "Mary, the mother of Jesus" i.e., (2). Mary Magdalene, and (3) the (third) Mary, the mother of James, the less and Joses (John 20. 25-27).

"Mary Magdalene," and Mary, the mother of Jesus and the other (third) Mary, followed Jesus from Galilee and ministered to him' This third Mary mother of James, the less, and Joses, (Mk. 15.40), was the woman that "asked Jesus to let her sons, i.e. "James, the less," and "Joses," sit on his "right and left," sides of his throne when came into his kingdom, for the special role she would later play in his resurrection.

Mary Magdalene, and the third Mary, mentioned together in very significance places in the gospels. Where other women are said to had witnessed things from afar, Mary Magdalene and third Mary are said to had "observed," where Jesus laid. (Mk. 15.40, 47). The third Mary and Mary Magdalene are always mention together in very important places in the gospel narrative, but unlike the other women who watch things from a distance Mary Magdalene and the third Mary are said to had been present at the cross of Jesus with his mother Mary and "the disciple Jesus loved." (John 19.25- 27).

When Joseph of Arimathea and Nicodemus (two secret disciples of Jesus) went to get Jesus's body, Pilate was very surprised that Jesus was dead so soon, because he only intended to "chastise, humiliate," and then release Jesus (Lk. 23.16, 17). The Jewish historian Joseph said he once knew a crucified man who lived three days on the cross and still was alive when they took him down from the cross. Jesus was crucified in the third hour, darkness came in the sixth hour and remained until the ninth hour when he cried out "My God, My God why have you forsaken me? according to the gospels of Matthew and Mark (Mt. 27.46; Mk. 15.34), while the Gospel of Luke says Jesus cried out "Father into your hands I commit my spirit," and he breathed his last." (Lk. 23.46). The Gospel of John describes the last words of Jesus to had been as follows.

"Now there stood by the cross of Jesus his mother, and his mother's sister (in-law) Mary the wife of Clopas, and Mary Magdalene. When Jesus therefore saw his mother, and the disciple whom he loved standing by, he said to his mother, "Woman, behold your son!" Then he said to the disciple, "Behold your mother!" And from that hour that disciple took her to his home." (John 19.25-27).

"After this, Jesus knowing that all things were now accomplished that the Scripture might be fulfilled, said "I thirst!" Now a vessel full of sour wine was sitting there; and they filled a sponge with sour wine, put on hyssop and put it to his mouth. So, when Jesus had received the sour wine, he said "It is finished," And bowing his head, he gave up his spirit." (John 19.28-30).

The disciple whom Jesus loved delivered the "sour wine," (infused with very strong medicine) that rendered Jesus him totally unconscious, and brain-dead, so he was non-responsive, when the soldiers came to break the legs of the those on the cross to accelerate their death, but thinking Jesus was already dead they did not break his legs, but one of the soldiers pierced his side with a spear, and immediately blood and water came out (Jesus unconscious but alive body) and they did not break his legs. (John 19.31-37). We now know blood and water won't flow out of "a dead body," and if blood and water ran out of Jesus' body, because he was still alive and his blood was circulating in his body.

Joseph of Arimathea, a rich man, who was once engaged to Mariamne II (Mary) and it is said he too was "waiting for the Kingdom of God to come, (Mk. 15.43) laid Jesus body in his newly designed and had craved cut tomb with a four square entrance open-face with a large circulate stone door that created a "gap," small "on the lower side small enough to require "the disciple Jesus loved," to have to "stood down," to see in but was large enough for Simon Peter to crawl in the tomb. (John 20.2-6).

The large circular stone door of Jesus' tomb, like others of its time never really fit perfectly and always created a gap between it and the actual tomb (large enough for the injured but alive Jesus crawl through). (comp.; Mt. 8.28-34; Mk. 5.1-4). Evidence indicate that Joseph of Arimathea and Nicodemus did not firmly seal the tomb with the large circulate stone and left a small gap on the lower side, threw which one stood down and look in, and Jesus could crawl through, the "gap," big enough for Peter to enter (John 20.5, 11, 12). And exchange places with the third Mary, sitting in front of the tomb of Jesus, with Mary Magdalene, waiting for the injured Jesus to ascend and exchange places with the third Mary sitting in front of the tomb. (Mt. 27.61; Mk. 5.1-2; Mt. 27.57-61).

All eyes were on the apostles who the Pharisees feared

might steal the body of Jesus, but they paid little or no attention to the females like Mary Magdalene and the third Mary, weeping and mourning in front of the tomb.

Nevertheless, when Jesus awoke from the (brain-dead) overdose he crawled out the small "gap," and exchanged places with (the third) Mary, who crawled into the tomb, where "she gracefully folded the "linen cloths," and the handkerchief," while she waited for the return of Mary Magdalene, to get her out the next morning before sunrise.

After Jesus' escape "tomb," the story was angelized by the Gospel of Matthew, saying "angel of the Lord," descended from heaven and came and roll back the stone from the door and sat on it," but the story was "angelized," to avoid revealing the identity of persons in involved, who could not be spoken of and allude to the truth (2 Cor. 12.4), that is that Joseph of Arimathea and Nicodemus (secret disciples of Jesus) left an opened gap for Jesus, whom they and laid the body of Jesus near the aired entrance "gap," could not be so openly stated. (2 Cor. 12.4).

The Essene Order of "Malchizedek," was the Order of the Angel of righteous, whose members dressed in "white apparel," made up the great cloud of cloud of witnesses of Mount Zion and to the city of the living God i.e. and received Jesus up into the mountain community of the Essene Order of Malchizedek. (Heb. 5.8-10; 12.1, 22, 33; Mt. 26.53)

when Jesus Christ ascended up in a great cloud of he told his disciples to remain in Jerusalem until the Holy

Spirit come upon them when he went to be nurse back to health on the of Pentecost. (Acts. 1.9- 11).

It came to past fifty days later on the day of Pentecost, when Jesus' health was restored, so much that when he awoke, the disciples felt his Spirit of his presence (again), and they were filed with "a holy spirit," themselves. The Pharisees, who denied Jesus resurrection also felt the Spirit of Jesus' presence, but could not find Jesus, because he had ascended into (the 3rd) heaven, and was received into a cloud of Essenes witnesses dressed in "white apparel," into their Community. (Acts 1.9-11; Heb. 5.10; 12.1, 22-23).

The Messiah of God, (the Christ), is "the Holy Spirit," (Gr. "to hagion to pneuma,") in human form. (Acts 2.33: Mt. 12.31; Mk. 3.28; Lk. 12.10).

On the day of Pentecost, the disciples felt the Spirit of the living presence of Jesus Christ and were themselves filled with "a holy spirit," (Greek, hagion pneuma) (Acts 2.4), erroneously render "the Holy Spirit," throughout the New Testament.(Acts 2.4) Later, in Chapter 2, Peter says, others could also receive "the gift of the Holy Spirit," i.e. "a holy spirit," (of their own) i.e. "that holy spirit of promised." (Acts 2.38, 39).

Nevertheless to continue, Pentecost phenomenon experience was likewise also felt by the high priest and the Pharisees who desired to find Jesus Christ "dead or "alive," and a man named Saul seeking fortune and fame persecuted Jesus' disciples but could not find him.

Chapter 3

TRANSFORMATION OF PAUL

The martyr of "Stephen," helped sheltered the disciples inconspicuously smuggling of Jesus out of Jerusalem, and the clothes laid at the feet of "Saul," (Acts 7.58). were used to provide the injured Jesus with a comfortable means of transportation on a small wooden wagon as he travelled to see his mother Mary (Mariamne II) in Damascus, at the house of the disciple called Judas (not Iscariot," and "the disciple whom Jesus loved,") in Damascus. (John 19.25-27).

"Saul," breathing threats against the disciples of Jesus went to the high priest and asked him for letters to the synagogue in Damascus to arrest Jesus'

mother and his younger brother, ("the disciple whom Jesus loved,") who lived Damascus. (Acts 9.11; John 19.25-27).

Saul persistence drove him to mistakenly catch up

with the disciples carrying Jesus to Damascus, (hidden under the clothes upon the wagon) and when approach them a light shone and Saul heard the voice from heaven say, "Saul, Saul why are you persecuting me?

Saul heard and asked who are you, Lord?" and Jesus removed the clothes covering him, set up and said "I am Jesus, whom you are persecuting. It is hard for you to kick against the goads," and it shocked Saul and caused him to fall off his horse and died.

Finding the letter from the high priest to the Damascus synagogue on "Saul's deceased body, they took the papers and Jesus assumed (the dead) Saul's identity and completed his quest to see his mother "Mary,"("Mariamne II,") in the house of Judas in Damascus on the street called "Straight," where the so-called "blind Saul," (the resurrected Jesus) was taken. (Acts 9.11; John 19.25-27).

According to the story, the Lord appeared in a vision to a disciple name "Ananias," (H6055, Anaiah, protected by God) was sent to heal the "Blind Saul," (the injured Jesus), who goes on to preach Christ in Damascus. (Acts 9.10-19). Saul (the resurrected Jesus Christ) later changed his name to "Paul," and while "Paul," (the resurrected Jesus Christ) grew stronger in seclusion, a powerful movement among the disciples at "Antioch," which cause the Jerusalem church to send "Joses, son of (third) Mary, who name they change to "Barnaba," (G921, son of prophecy) and sent on a special mission to "Antioch," and "needing assistance," he went and got Paul (the resurrected Jesus) and brought him (the resurrected Jesus Christ) to Antioch in about 44 A.D. There Paul (the resurrected Jesus Christ) ministered to the disciples, saying;

"It is doubtless not profitable for me to boast. I will come to visions and revelations of the Lord: I knew a man in Christ fourteen years ago—whether in the body I do not know, whether out of the body I do not know but God know—how such a man— whether in the body or out of the body I do not know, God knows—how he was caught up into "Paradise," (i.e. the third heaven), and heard inexpressible words, which it is not lawful for a man to utter. Of such a one I will boast; yet of myself I will not boast, except in my infirmities. For though I might desire to be boast, I will be no fool; for I will speak the truth. But I refrain, lest anyone should think of me above what he sees of me to be or hears from me." (2 Cor. 12.1-6). Here "Paul," (the resurrected Jesus Christ) alludes to his (Jesus) ascension into heaven, i.e. the heavenly community of the Essene's Order of Malchizedek (Heb. 5.8-10; 12.1, 22, 23). Paul (Jesus) next speaks of the injured he received during crucifixion, saying "And lest I should be exalted above measure by the abundance of revelations, a thorn in the flesh was given to me, a message of Satan to buffet me, lest I be exalted above measure. Concerning this I pleaded with the Lord three times that it might depart from me.

And he said to me, "My grace is sufficient for you, for My strength is made perfect in weakness (2 Cor. 12.7-9).

Here Paul (Jesus) alludes the soldier piercing "Jesus," (Paul) in the side to insure he was dead. (John 19.34). The "thorn in Paul's in the side came from Jesus' body being pierced in his side by the soldier (2 Cor. 12.7; John 19.34). Nevertheless, Paul (Jesus) having had his hands also pierced manage to handwrite the Epistle of Galatians in his own hand (Gal. 6.11, 12). Elsewhere, Paul (the resurrected Jesus Christ) states: "For now we see through a glass, darkly; but then face to face: now I know in part; but then shall I know even as also I am known. (1 Cor. 13.12).

Chapter 4

THE WRITING OF THE NEW TESTAMENT

The Apostle Paul (the resurrected Jesus Christ) dictated or ordered the contents of all the epistles, and also dictated all four Gospels. "Joses," one of the two sons of the (third) Mary, who was at the cross and the tomb of Jesus, and had asked that her two sons "James, the less, and Joses sit on his right and left sides for her participation in Jesus resurrection, i.e. "Joses."

The Jerusalem disciples changed her son "Joses," name to "Barnabas," (G921, son of prophecy) and instructed him to accompanied Paul (Jesus) on the first ministry journey.

On this first ministry journey Barnabas brought with him his young cousin "John Mark," the scribe of the Gospel of Mark, first written gospel, which was being written during this first missionary journey by the dictates of the apostle Paul (the resurrected Jesus Christ).

However, when there arose a serious contention between the Apostle Paul (the resurrected Jesus) and John Mark, the conflict resulted in Mark returning home to Jerusalem. (Acts 13.13; 15.36-41).

The texts suggest the disagreement was over the young Mark's desire "to literally write of the life and death of Jesus," but the apostles Paul (the resurrected Jesus) desire to "angelized," the stories to conceal the names and acts of people of whom it was not lawful to speak. (2 Cor. 12.7-9).

It appears the younger John Mark favored "a more literal writing," of the gospel story, but the older Apostle Paul (the resurrected Jesus) preferred a more "angelized," version of those things, because he had been caught up into Paradise and heard inexpressible words which is not lawful for a man to utter." (2 Cor. 12.4).

In the Gospel of Mark, one finds no mention of "the cost of being a disciple," which is found in both Matthew's and Luke's gospel, which alludes to Mark returning to Jerusalem. (Mt. 8.19-22; Lk. 9.62; Acts 13.13, 15.38).

In the Gospel of Mark, the only mention of "angels," are in the mouth of Jesus who said, "In the resurrection the believers who be like "angels," (Mk. 12.25) and then he will send "his angels," and gather his elect from the four winds, from the farthest parts of earth to the earth to the farthest parts of heaven." (Mk. 13.27). "But of that day and hour no one knows not even the angels in heaven nor the Son but only the Father." (Mk. 13.32).

After the split between Mark and the Apostle Paul (the resurrected Jesus), the position of scribe held was filled by Matthew and in later years by Luke, the physician.

Both Matthew and Luke supply dramatically different dates for the birth of Jesus, and both are "angelized," with many mentions of angels (spirits) doing things.

The Gospel of John mentions "angels in human form," i.e. An angel of the Essene Commune went down at a certain time and stirred the waters (Gen. 5.4; 12.29).

The Gospel of Mathews mentions, "the angel of the Lord," five times, and tells us Mary (Mariamne II) the virgin daughter of a priest from Egypt, called "Simeon," and that she was betrothed to Joseph of Arimathea when they were young, but king Herod sexually defiled her, and to appease the anger of her father (Simeon) and the Jews King Herod made her father "Simeon," high priest and ordered the rebuilding of the temple which began in 20 B.C. (Dan. 9.26, 27)

The angelized story supplied in the Gospel of Matthew 4 B. C. alludes to the time the dying king Herod ordered Mariamne II be killed, and of Joseph rescuing her and taking her to Egypt until King Herod died in 4 B.C., and also alludes to the 15-year old Jesus making his first violent effort to seize the throne of Judea ruled by Herod (who fathered him) as "Theudas," (who) "boasting himself to be somebody; to whom a number of men about four hundred joined themselves; was slain and all as many as obeyed him, were scattered, and brought to naught." (Acts 5.36).

While he (Joseph) thought about these things, behold an angel of the Lord (i.e. Simeon) told him that "conceived in her is of the Holy Spirit." (Mt. 1.20). "Then Joseph being aroused from sleep, did as the angel the angel of the Lord (Simeon) commanded him and took to him his wife, Mariamne II, (Mary)" (Mt. 1.24) When they departed angel of the Lord (Simeon) told Joseph to take Mariamne II (Mary) to Egypt, and they remained until Herod died in 4 B.C.

It is known Herod died in 4 B.C. so biblical scholars assume Jesus had to be been born before his death. However, we know the Messiah had to be born when the temple was rebuilt according to prophecy which occurred in 20 B.C. when king Herod ordered the rebuilding of the temple and made Simeon high priest and ordered the rebuilding to appease their anger for him having sexually defiling his daughter "Mariamne II," the daughter of Simeon. (Dan. 9.25, 26).

What did happen in 4 B.C. right before the death of Herod, he ordered the murder of Mariamne II (Mary) Jesus' mother, when the 15-year-old Jesus learned of these things caused him to make his first violent attempt to seize the throne of Judea, as "Theudas," (Acts 5.36).

Likewise, the Gospel of Luke, suggest a 6 A.D. date for Jesus' birth, alludes to Jesus second attempt to violently seize the throne of Judea as Judas of Galilee in the days of taxing in about 6 A.D. when Jesus was about 26 years old (Lk. 2.1; Acts 5.37).

Thereafter, Jesus entered into seclusion for about 18 years in the wilderness where he studied the scriptures and mastered the Old Testament scriptures teachings and revelations. After seriously considering "facing the cross as the Son of man," character and the demands on everything occurring in a time in the tomb to be conveniently close, and knowing what must be done came forth with the grace of God upon him, he left the wilderness and resurfaced as John the Baptist, seeing to Baptize everyone, especially the Messiah who was to come.

After the wilderness express, "Jesus," re- surfaced as "John, the Baptist," searching to baptize the Messiah when "The Spirit of God," descended upon him, and caused to change his identity from John, the Baptist to the Messiah "Jesus Christ," who knew a conspiracy was made against him the "green olive tree," and yet he held his peace (Jer. 11.9, 16- 19).

The conspiracy to make the Messiah Jesus Christ a human sacrifice for the sins of the world, so as to cause all to worship the "new Babylonian-god of Cyrus, the great," under the name "Jehovah," (the Lord) but Jesus Christ being fully aware of the conspiracy also organized away of overcoming crucifixion and prearranged his resurrection from the tomb, on the third day.

After his resurrection Jesus Christ proceeded to assuming the identity of the Apostle Paul, (the resurrected Jesus Christ), who dictated all four gospels, and the epistles or directed their contents, restored the ancient prophecy and prepared the mystery of his return, before the 88 year old the resurrect Jesus Christ, under the identity of the Apostle Paul (Heb. 3.1) was decapitated by Nero in 68 A.D. which initiated the uprising that resulted the destruction of the temple in 70 A. D.

"For I am now ready to be offered and the time of my departure is at hand. I have finished my course, I have kept the faith: Henceforth there is laid up for me a crown of righteousness, which the Lord, the righteous judge, shall give me at that day: and not to me only but unto all them also that "respects," his appearing." (2 Tim. 4.6-8).

When reliable witnesses confirmed the demise of the Apostle Paul (the resurrected Jesus Christ) (Heb. 3.1), it initiated the uprising that resulted in the destruction of the temple built by king Herod, when Jesus Christ was born, in 20 B.C.

Chapter 5

THE TEACHINGS OF JESUS CHRIST

After his resurrection Jesus appeared three times, during the third occasion Jesus asked Peter (1). Simon, son of Jonah, "do you "agape," (G25) more than these and Peter responded saying "Yes Lord you know that I "phileo," (G5368) and Jesus responded "Feed my Lambs (John 21.15). Again, a second time (2). Jesus asked Peter again "do you "Agape," (G25), and again Peter said to Jesus, "Yo know that "phileo," (G5368) and Jesus said to him "Tend my sheep (John 21.16).

Next, the third time (3). Jesus uses Peter's word "phileo," (G5368) and proceeds to asked Peter "do you "phileo," (G5368), and Peter was grieved because Jesus said to him the third time, "Do you "phileo," Me?" and Jesus said to him "Feed my sheep," (John 21.17).

. The word "love," appears in the New Testament at

about 175 times, and the vast majority of times it is used to translate the Greek word "agape," (G26). However, the Greek texts in about 18 verses, the Greek "phileo," (G5368) is used and translated "love,"

The Greek "phileo," is made up of the Greek "phi," the 21st letter of the Old Greek alphabet which later replaced by "v," the 22 letter of the modern English alphabet, causing the word "phileo," to read "vleo," which was thereafter punned to create the word "love," which has the meaning "affection." Early Christians not knowing the true meaning of the word "agape," applied the meaning "affection." like "phileo," from which came.

"When you pray, you shall not be like the hypocrites. For they love (G5368, phileo) to pray standing in the synagogues, and on the corners of the streets, that they may be seen by men. Assuredly. I say to you, they have their reward. (Mt. 6.5).

"They love (G5368, phileo) the beast places at the synagogues. (Mt. 23.6). And because lawlessness will abound, the love (G5368, phileo) of many will grow cold." (Mt. 24.12). "Beware of the scribes who desire to go around in long robes, love (phileo) greetings in the marketplaces the beat seats in the synagogues and the best places at feasts." (Lk. 20.38). "if you were of the world, the world would love (phileo) its own..." (John 15.19). Added to this short list is the couple times "Phileo," is used by Peter when he was talking to Jesus. (John 21.16, 17). The word "phileo," is translated "love," several more times in the epistles indicating the same kind of "affection." However, in the epistle to First Corinthians chapter 13, the so-called "Love chapter," the Greek "phileo," (G G5368) does not appear. Therein the Greek word translated "love," is "agape." The first Timothy chapter 1, alludes to the conflict caused these two words and speaks of the correct understanding and application of the terms translated "love," saying;

"Now the purpose of the commandment is "agape," (love) from a pure heart, from a good conscience and from sincere faith, from which some having strayed, have turned to Idle talk. Desiring to be teachers of the law, understanding neither what they say nor the things which they affirm. But we know that the law is good if one uses it lawfully. Knowing this that the law is not made for a righteous person, but for the lawless and insubordinate, for the ungodly and for sinners, for the unholy and profane, for murders of fathers and murders of mothers, for manslayers. For fornicators, for sodomites, for kidnappers, for liars, for perjurers, and if there is any other thing that is contrary to sound doctrine, according to the glorious gospel of the blessed God which was committed to my trust." (1 Tim. 1.5-11).

Whenever, the word "agape," appears in a verse next to the word "Philadelphia," (brotherly love), agape is erroneously rendered "charity," (affection), and

"Philadelphia," is rendered "brotherly kindness." The etymology of the Greek "agape," may be correctly traced back to the Hebrew word, "agab," (H5689) which denotes a strong inordinate sexual love desire, that the new Greek converts were familiar. However, "agape," was used to translate the Hebrew word "Ahab," (H157) which has been defined "love." However, the etymologies of "Ahab," show it is a contraction of the Hebrew word "achab," (uncle) which means "brother (or friend) of father." According to tradition, the children were to show same (none sexual) "love and respect," they had for their father to his "brother," or "friend." Hence, "Ahab," means (love and respect), but essentially denotes "respect,' in that the children were to show the same "(love) and respect," they had for the father to their father's brother or friend. All of which are essentially incorporated in the definition "respect." This can be easily seen in the contexts and use of the Hebrew "Ahab," and the Greek "agape," its equivalent.

For example, in Romans 14.15, the biblical scholars the word "agape," is erroneously translated "charitably," but it should more correctly rendered "respectfully," and read as follows: "If your brother be grieved with your meat, now walk you not "respectfully." Destroy not him with your meat, for whom Christ died." (Rom. 14.15). "Above all these things put on "respect," which is the bond of perfectness." (Col. 3.14). Flee also youthful lusts; but follow righteousness, faith, "respect," peace, with them that call on the Lord out of a pure heart." (2 Tim. 2.22).

"And above all things have fervent "respect," among yourselves; for "respect," shall cover the multitude of sins." (1 Pet. 4.8). "to brotherly kindness," (add) "respect," (2 Pet. 1.7). "These are spots in your feasts of Respect, when they feast with you, feeding themselves without fear." (Jude 1.12).

Now the end of the commandment is "respect," (G26) out of a pure heart, and of a good conscience, and of faith unfeigned." (1 Tim. 1.5). The "doctrine of first mention," says that the first time a word is mentioned in the scripture, the context itself will indicate the word's meaning. The first time the word "agape," (respect) is in Matthew chapter 5. 43-48, which reads as follows:

"You have heard that it was said "You shall "respect," your neighbor and hate your enemy. But I say to you, "respect," your enemies, bless those who curse you, do good to those who hate you, and pray for those who spitefully use you and persecute you. That you may be sons of your Father in heaven; for He makes his sun rise on the evil and on the good, and send rain on the just and the unjust. For if you "respect," those who respect you, what reward have you? Do not even the tax collectors do the same? And if you greet your brethren only, what do you do more than others? Do not even the tax collectors do so? Therefore, you shall be perfect just as your Father in heaven is perfect." (Mt. 5.43-48).

It ultimately clear from the text God is not a respecter of person and that He respect all, and that the word "agape," means "respect." In Mark chapter 12 and Matthew chapter 22, a lawyer of the Pharisees, asked Jesus what was the greatest commandment. And he answered saying the first and greatness commandment was "You shall "respect," the Lord your God with all your heart, with all your heart, with all your soul and with all your mind. This is the first and great commandment. And the second is like it: You shall respect your neighbor as yourself. (Mk. 12.28-34).

In the Gospel of Luke, we don't have the two great commandments, instead we are given we are given the "parable of the Good Samaritan. This story tells the story of a Jewish man who was attacked and stripped of all his clothes and left for dead. A priest and a Levite passed by but would not stop to help their Jewish brethren, but later a Samaritan. (with whom the Jews have no dealing no dealings with the Samaritans), yet one stopped and helped him, and to him to the inn and payed the cost of taking care of this Jewish man. The question is why? and the answer is the Samaritan had a "respect," for life, a concept not shared once shared the Jews.

Looking, to the 10 commandments one finds the first four commandments addresses man relationship between God and mankind, and the remaining six commandments address mam relationship with man, but they all mandate "respect." Turning to the so-called "Love Chapter,"

1 Corinthians Chapter 13, in which the word "agape," is erroneously rendered "love," (affection) and/or "charity," (affection). As stated and shown "agape," is the Greek equivalent of the Hebrew "Ahab," which comes from the Hebrew word "achab," for "uncle," i.e. "brother (friend) of father," because the children were to show him the same "respect, (love and respect) their showed to their father. 1 Corinthians 13, should be more correctly be read and understood as follows:

"Though I speak with the tongues of men and of angels, but have not "respect," I have become sounding brass or clanging cymbal. And though I have the gift of prophecy, and understand all mysteries and all knowledge, and though I have all faith, so that I could remove mountains, but have not "respect," I am nothing. And though I bestow all my goods to feed the poor, and though I give my body to be burned, but have not "respect," it profits me nothing.

"Respect," does not envy, "respect," does not parade itself, is not puffed up. Dose not behave rudely, does not seek its own, is not provoked, thinks no evil, dose not rejoice in iniquity but rejoices in the truth; bears all things, believes all things, hope all thing, endures all things.

"Respect," never fails, but whether there are prophecies, they will fail; whether there are tongues, they will cease; whether there is knowledge, it will vanish away.

For we know in part and we prophesy in part. But when that which is "perfect," (G5046, mature), has come, then that which is in part will be done away.

When I was a child, I spoke as a child, as a child, I thought as a child; but when I became a man, I put away childish things. For now, we see in a mirror, dimly, but then face to face, Now I know in part, but then I shall know "just as I also am known.

And now abide in faith, hope, and "respect," these three; but the greatest of these is "respect."

Agape- Maran-atha, Thaddeus Michael Lebbeus

THE INDEX